Ketogenic Crock Pot

Cookbook

50 Amazing Recipes from Beginners to advanced.
Learn How to lose weight fast, reset metabolism and
Regain confidence with Foolproof & wholesome recipes

Clara Smith

Table of Contents

Introduction

The crockpot has long been a favorite kitchen implement for the 'set-it-and-forget-it' meal. It's a wonderful invention by whoever thought it up, and it has saved many a few dollars on electricity by not needing to keep the stove and oven on for extended hours and all day. So, what really is a crockpot?

The crockpot slow cooking method involves basically depositing the ingredients you desire to cook into the crockpot bowl (usually by stirring it with a wooden spoon or a ladle), adding the liquid of choice, cooking it for a few hours until it's done. These used to be the standard cooking methods in kitchens, and they have stayed the same with the invention of the crockpot. Nowadays, most crockpots have interiors thermostatically controlled to ensure that it's set at the right temperature during the cooking process to not over-cook your meals.

The best in crockpot slow cooking is finding that low and slow recipe. Recipes that are low in time length are usually very low in steps, and not much work is involved. It usually leads to the much sought after 'set it and forget it' kind of meal. Imagine not having to watch your meals cook slowly as you work on other tasks; you can avoid the temptation of peeking or checking on it too often and not having to worry about burning or crusting on the sides of your crockpot. When cooking at low heat, you don't have to worry about your meal exploding all over the kitchen or all the grease falling out and sticking to the bottom of your crock.

The best use of crockpot slow cooking is the convenience of the food, especially during holidays and parties. You can set the crockpot down on the table, and everyone can serve themselves. It is an excellent and great way to spend time with your guests and treat them well. There is nothing cheesier than eating the same dish fondue style. You get to enjoy slow cooking hotdogs for hours and hours without little ones surreptitiously taking off the top and poaching them in the pool of oil sitting beside the dish.

A crockpot is a very good way to use leftovers for a delicious meal. If you cook a large meal regularly and you have leftovers, put them in a crockpot with a liquid and let it cook. It will double the amount of food leftover or fed to the cat at the end of the week.

Crockpot cooking generally saves time, but it is also a low-budget way to cook. Slow cooking food can save you money because they are usually very low and easy to make. In fact, it is even possible to cook a meal with the last few pennies in your wallet. If you're on a tight budget and you don't have much to spend on your meals, the crockpot is the way to go.

Crockpots even make for a great gift since it's made in many shapes and sizes, from the really small, 1-quart crockpot to the huge 8 quarts or more. Any shape or size would be a welcome gift for anyone because everyone eats. Any occasion could be a good time to give someone a crockpot, and the more occasions you can name, the more crockpots you could make as gifts.

Crockpots are a good thing for singles who do not have many friends, and getting together can be difficult. You can go on cooking and not having to worry about cooking for anyone. You also don't have to go through the motions of doing a dinner party or charity work every week. You could just throw some ingredients together in your crockpot, turn it on and leave. That way, you're free to do whatever you like while your crockpot cooks your meal.

To whom is this cookbook? This cookbook is for people who want to spend less time in the kitchen and less money on food. This cookbook is also for people who wish to cook their meals in a healthy manner or for people with little time or money, and lastly, this is for people who enjoy sharing meals with friends and family. Treat your guests to a good meal every day. Slow cooking, live long!

CHAPTER 1:

Breakfast

1.   Scrambled Eggs in Ramekins

Preparation time: 5 minutes

Cooking time: 4 hours

Servings: 2

Ingredients:

- 2 eggs, beaten

- ¼ cup milk

- Salt and pepper

- ¼ cup cheddar cheese, grated

- ½ cup salsa

Directions:

1. In a mixing bowl, mix the eggs and milk. Season with salt and pepper to taste. Place egg mixture in two ramekins. Sprinkle with cheddar cheese on top.

2. Place the ramekins in the crockpot and pour water around it. Close the lid and cook on low for 4 hours. Serve with salsa.

Nutrition:

Calories: 243

Carbohydrates: 9.3g

Protein: 15.3g

Fat: 164g

2.   Bacon Hash Brown and Egg Casserole

Preparation time: 10 minutes

Cooking time: 6 hours

Servings: 7

Ingredients:

- 1 package hash brown potatoes, thawed

- 8 large eggs, beaten 1 can evaporated milk

- 2 cups sharp cheddar cheese, grated

- 1 package bacon, cooked until crispy

Directions:

1. Place the hash brown potatoes in the crockpot. In a mixing bowl, mix the eggs and milk together. Season with salt and pepper to taste. Pour the egg mixture over the hash brown potatoes. Sprinkle with cheddar

cheese. Sprinkle with bacon on top. Close the lid and cook on low for 6 hours.

Nutrition: Calories: 269 Carbohydrates: 13.8g Protein: 13.6g Fat: 17.5g

3.   Crockpot Veggie Omelet

Preparation time: 5 minutes

Cooking time: 6 hours

Servings: 6

Ingredients:

- 6 eggs, beaten

- ½ cup milk

- 1 teaspoon seasoning of your choice (thyme or dried basil) 2 red and yellow bell peppers, julienned

- 1 cup broccoli florets

Directions:

1. In a mixing bowl, combine the eggs, milk, and seasoning of your choice. Season with salt and pepper to taste.

2. Pour the egg mixture into the crockpot. Add the vegetables on top. Close the lid and cook on low for 6 hours. Serve with cheese if desired.

Nutrition: Calories: 144 Carbohydrates: 2.3g Protein: 9.4g Fat: 10.7g

4.   Enchilada Breakfast Casserole

Preparation time: 5 minutes

Cooking time: 10 hours

Servings: 8

Ingredients:

- 6 eggs, beaten 1-pound ground beef

- 2 cans enchilada sauce

- 1 can condensed cream of onion soup

- 3 cups sharp cheddar cheese, grated

Directions:

1. In a mixing bowl, beat the eggs and season with salt and pepper. Set aside. In a skillet, brown the beef for at least 5 minutes.

2. Pour the beef in the crockpot and stir in the enchilada sauce and cream of onion soup. Stir in the eggs and place cheese on top. Close the lid and cook on low for 10 hours.

Nutrition: Calories: 320 Carbohydrates: 9.4g Protein: 24.6g Fat: 20.1g

5.   White Chocolate Oatmeal

Preparation time: 5 minutes

Cooking time: 4 hours Servings: 6

Ingredients:

- 1 tablespoon white chocolate chips

- 1 cup water ½ cup oatmeal

- 1 tablespoon brown sugar

- 1 teaspoon cinnamon

Directions:

1. Stir in all ingredients in the crockpot. Close the lid and cook on low for 4 hours. Top with your favorite topping.

Nutrition: Calories: 31 Carbohydrates: 5.4g Protein: 0.5g Fat: 0.9g

CHAPTER 2:

Mains

6.   Autumnal Stew

Preparation time: 15 minutes Cooking time: 6 hours

Servings: 6

Ingredients:

- 4 cups butternut squash cubes

- 1 shallot, chopped

- 2 garlic cloves, chopped

- 2 red apples, peeled and diced

- 1 celery stalk, sliced

- 1 carrot, sliced

- 2 ripe tomatoes, peeled and diced

- 1/4 teaspoon cumin powder

- 1 pinch chili powder

- 1/2 cup tomato sauce

- 1/2 cup vegetable stock

- Salt and pepper to taste

Directions:

1. Combine all the ingredients in your Crock Pot. Add salt and pepper to taste and cook on low settings for 6 hours. Serve the stew warm and fresh.

Nutrition:

Calories: 177 Carbs: 15g Fat: 4g Protein: 21g

7.   Turnip and Beans Casserole

Preparation time: 15 minutes

Cooking time: 6 hours

Servings: 4

Ingredients:

- ½ cup turnip, chopped 1 teaspoon chili powder

- ¼ cup of coconut milk 1 teaspoon coconut oil

- ¼ cup potato, chopped 1 carrot, diced

- 1 cup red kidney beans, canned

- ½ cup Cheddar cheese, shredded

Directions:

1. Grease the Crock Pot bottom with coconut oil. Then put the turnip and potato inside. Sprinkle the vegetables with chili powder and coconut milk.

2. After this, top the with red kidney beans and Cheddar cheese. Close the lid and cook the casserole on Low for 6 hours.

Nutrition: Calories 266 Protein 14.5g Carbohydrates 31.4g Fat 10g

8.   Quinoa Black Bean Chili

Preparation time: 15 minutes

Cooking time: 6 hours

Servings: 6

Ingredients:

- 1/2 cup quinoa, rinsed

- 1 can (15 oz.) black beans, drained

- 1 can fire roasted tomatoes

- 1 sweet onion, chopped

- 2 garlic cloves, chopped

- 1 1/2 cups vegetable stock

- 1/4 teaspoon chili powder

- 1/4 teaspoon cumin powder

- Salt and pepper to taste

Directions:

1. Combine the quinoa, black beans, tomatoes, onion, garlic and stock, as well as chili powder and cumin powder. Season with salt and pepper and cook on low settings for 6 hours. Serve the chili warm.

Nutrition:

Calories: 317

Carbs: 44g

Fat: 9g

Protein: 15g

9.   Collard Greens Stew

Preparation time: 15 minutes

Cooking time: 6 hours Servings: 6

Ingredients:

- 1 tablespoon olive oil 2 garlic cloves, chopped

- 1 cup dried black beans, rinsed 1/2 cup tomato sauce

- 2 cups vegetable stock 1 bunch collard greens, shredded Salt and pepper to taste 1 tablespoon chopped cilantro for serving

Directions:

1. Combine all the ingredients in your crock pot, adding salt and pepper as needed. Cook on low settings for 6 hours. Serve the stew warm and fresh or chilled.

Nutrition: Calories: 76 Carbs: 13g Fat: 1g Protein: 5g

10. Shredded Pork with Beans

Preparation Time: 5 minutes

Cooking Time: 8 hours Servings: 10

Ingredients:

- 3 pounds pork tenderloin, cut into large chunks

- 2 cans black beans, drained

- 1 jar picante sauce 1 teaspoon oregano

- Salt and pepper to taste

Directions:

1. Place all ingredients in a mixing bowl. Place all ingredients in the crockpot. Close the lid and cook on low for 8 hours. Serve with rice if desired.

Nutrition: Calories: 207 Carbohydrates: 14g Protein: 26g Fat: 4g

11. Mexican Bubble Pizza

Preparation Time: 10 minutes

Cooking Time: 10 hours

Servings: 7

Ingredients:

- 1 ½ pounds ground beef 1 can condensed tomato soup

- 1 envelope taco seasoning

- 1 tube buttermilk biscuits

- 2 cups cheddar cheese, grated

Directions:

1. Heat skillet over medium-high heat and brown the ground beef for a few minutes. Place in the crockpot.

2. Add the tomato soup and taco seasoning. Season with salt and pepper to taste. Place the buttermilk biscuits on top and sprinkle with cheddar cheese. Close the lid and cook on low for 10 hours.

Nutrition:Calories: 643 Carbohydrates: 46g Protein: 35g Fat: 35g

12.   Tender Turkey Breasts

Preparation Time: 5 minutes

Cooking Time: 8 hours Servings: 12

Ingredients:

- 6 pounds turkey breasts, bone-in

- ½ cup water 1 tablespoon brown sugar

- 4 cloves of garlic, minced

- 4 sprigs rosemary

Directions:

1. Place all ingredients in a mixing bowl. Place all ingredients in the crockpot. Close the lid and cook on low for 8 hours.

Nutrition: Calories: 318 Carbohydrates: 2g Protein: 47g Fat: 12g

CHAPTER 3:

Sides

13. Carrot and Beet Side Salad

Preparation time: 15 minutes

Cooking Time: 7 Hours Servings: 6

Ingredients:

- ½ cup walnuts, chopped

- ¼ cup lemon juice

- ½ cup olive oil

- 1 shallot, chopped

- 1 teaspoon Dijon mustard

- 1 tablespoon brown sugar

- Salt and black pepper to the taste

- 2 beets, peeled and cut into wedges

- 2 carrots, peeled and sliced

- 1 cup parsley

- 5 ounces arugula

Directions:

1. In your Crock Pot, mix beets with carrots, salt, pepper, sugar, mustard, shallot, oil, lemon juice and walnuts, cover and cook on Low for 7 hours.

2. Transfer everything to a bowl, add parsley and arugula, toss, divide between plates and serve as a side dish.

Nutrition: Calories 100 Fat 3g Carbs 7g Protein 3g

14.   Asparagus and Mushroom Mix

Preparation time: 15 minutes

Cooking Time: 5 Hours Servings: 4

Ingredients:

- 2 pounds asparagus spears, cut into medium pieces

- 1 cup mushrooms, sliced A drizzle of olive oil

- Salt and black pepper to the taste

- 2 cups coconut milk

- 1 teaspoon Worcestershire sauce

- 5 eggs, whisked

Directions:

1. Grease your Crock Pot with the oil and spread asparagus and mushrooms on the bottom.

2. In a bowl, mix the eggs with milk, salt, pepper and Worcestershire sauce, whisk, pour into the Crock Pot, toss everything, cover and cook on Low for 6 hours. Divide between plates and serve as a side dish.

Nutrition:

Calories 211

Fat 4g

Carbs 6g

Protein 5g

15.   Garlic Mushrooms

Preparation time: 15 minutes

Cooking Time: 8 hours

Servings: 6

Ingredients:

- 2 lbs. cremini mushrooms, quartered

- 1 lemon, chopped

- ½ cup fresh parsley

- 1 tsp salt

- 1 tsp ground black pepper

- 1/3 cup half and half

- 1 tsp thyme

- 1 tsp coriander

- 1 tsp turmeric

- 3 tbsp garlic, chopped

Directions:

1. Spread the mushrooms in the insert of Crock Pot. Whisk the half and half cream with remaining ingredients.

2. Top the mushrooms with the cream sauce. Put the crock pot's lid on and set the cooking time to 8 hours on Low settings. Serve warm.

Nutrition:

Calories: 55

Fat: 0.8g

Carbs: 9.43g

Protein: 6g

16. Jalapeno Meal

Preparation time: 15 minutes

Cooking Time: 6 hours

Servings: 6

Ingredients:

- 12 oz. jalapeno pepper, cut in half and deseeded

- 2 tbsp olive oil 1 tbsp balsamic vinegar

- 1 onion, sliced 1 garlic clove, sliced

- 1 tsp ground coriander

- 4 tbsp water

Directions:

1. Place the jalapeno peppers in the Crock Pot. Top the pepper with olive oil, balsamic vinegar, onion, garlic, coriander, and water.

2. Put the crock pot's lid on and set the cooking time to

6 hours on Low settings. Serve warm.

Nutrition: Calories: 67 Fat: 4.7g Carbs: 6.02g Protein: 1g

17. Dill Mixed Fennel

Preparation time: 15 minutes

Cooking Time: 3 Hours

Servings: 7

Ingredients:

- 10 oz. fennel bulbs, diced

- 2 tbsp olive oil

- 1 tsp ground black pepper

- 1 tsp paprika

- 1 tsp cilantro

- 1 tsp oregano

- 1 tsp basil

- 3 tbsp white wine

- 1 tsp salt

- 2 garlic cloves

- 1 tsp dried dill

Directions:

1. Add fennel bulbs and all other ingredients to the Crock Pot. Put the crock pot's lid on and set the cooking time to 3 hours and 30 minutes on High settings. Serve warm.

Nutrition:

Calories: 53

Fat: 4.1g

Carbs: 4g

Protein: 1g

CHAPTER 4:

Seafood

18. Luscious Herbed Clams

Preparation Time: 10 minutes

Cooking Time: 2 hours

Servings: 12

Ingredients:

- 1 tablespoon of oregano, dried

- ½ cup of butter

- 2 cups of white wine

- 1 teaspoon of red pepper flakes

- 1 teaspoon of fresh parsley, roughly diced

- 36 clams, scrubbed

- 5 garlic cloves, peeled and minced

Directions:

1. Start by throwing all the fixings into your Crockpot. Cover its lid and cook for 2 hours on Low setting. Once done, remove its lid and give it a stir. Serve warm.

Nutrition:

Calories 455

Fat 34.4 g

Carbs 10.8 g

Protein 29.6 g

19. Cider Soaked Pancetta Clams

Preparation Time: 10 minutes

Cooking Time: 2 hours

Servings: 6

Ingredients:

- 3 oz. pancetta

- 2 lbs. clams, scrubbed

- 1 tablespoon of olive oil

- Juice from ½ lemon

- 1 bottle infused cider

- 3 tablespoons of butter

- Salt and black pepper ground, to taste

- 2 garlic cloves, peeled and diced

- 2 thyme sprigs, diced

Directions:

1. Start by throwing all the fixings into your Crockpot. Cover its lid and cook for 2 hours on Low setting. Once done, remove its lid and give it a stir. Serve warm.

Nutrition:

Calories 355

Fat 15 g

Carbs 11.8 g

Protein 44.2 g

20.   Scallops with Romanesco

Preparation Time:10 minutes

Cooking Time:1 hour

Servings: 4

Ingredients:

- 1/2 Romanesco head, trimmed

- 3 tablespoon of olive oil

- 1 cup of chicken stock

- 1 tablespoon of butter

- 1 shallot, peeled and diced

- 3 garlic cloves, peeled and minced

- 1 lb. scallops

- 2 cups of spinach, chopped

- ¼ cup of walnuts, toasted and diced

- 1½ cups of pomegranate seeds

- Salt and black pepper ground, to taste

Directions:

1. Start by throwing all the fixings into your Crockpot. Cover its lid and cook for 1 hour on Low setting. Once done, remove its lid and give it a stir. Serve warm.

Nutrition:

Calories 307

Fat 29 g

Carbs 7 g

Protein 6 g

21.   Jalapeno Cheese Oysters

Preparation Time: 10 minutes

Cooking Time: 2 hours

Servings: 9

Ingredients:

- 1 jalapeño pepper, diced

- 2 tomatoes, cored and diced

- 18 oysters, scrubbed

- 2 limes, cut into wedges

- ½ cup of fresh cilantro, diced

- Salt and black pepper ground, to taste

- ½ cup of Monterey Jack cheese, shredded

- ¼ cup of onion, diced

- ½ cup of vegetable stock

- Juice from 1 lime

Directions:

1. Start by throwing all the fixings into your Crockpot. Cover its lid and cook for 2 hours on Low setting. Once done, remove its lid and give it a stir. Serve warm.

Nutrition:

Calories 487

Fat 37.4 g

Carbs 10.6 g

Protein 28.1 g

22.   Salmon with Mushroom

Preparation Time: 10 minutes

Cooking Time: 3 hours

Servings: 4

Ingredients:

- ¼ cup of mayonnaise

- 2 salmon fillets

- 2 cups of spinach, chopped

- A drizzle of olive oil

- 6 mushrooms, diced

- ¼ cup of macadamia nuts, toasted and roughly diced

- 3 green onions, diced

- Salt and black pepper ground, to taste

- A pinch of nutmeg

- 5 oz. tiger shrimp, peeled, deveined, and diced

Directions:

1. Start by throwing all the fixings into your Crockpot except shrimp. Cover its lid and cook for 2 hours on High setting.

2. Once done, remove its lid and give it a stir. Stir in shrimp and continue cooking for 1 hour on low heat. Serve warm.

Nutrition:

Calories 282

Fat 4.6 g

Carbs 11.1 g

Protein 22.2 g

CHAPTER 5:

Poultry

23. Chicken Stock

Preparation time: 15 minutes

Cooking time: 6-8 hours

Servings: 1

Ingredients:

- 3 pounds chicken cut to pieces

- 1 liter water

- 2 ribs of thickly sliced celery

- 3 thickly sliced small onions

- 3 medium carrots

- 1 small turnip, cut into 4 pieces

- Garlic (5 cloves)

- 1 teaspoon dried sage leaves

- 2 bay leaves

- 1/2 teaspoon whole peppercorns

- Salt and pepper

Directions:

1. Mix all the ingredients other than salt and pepper, in a crock pot. Cover and cook on low 6 to 8 hours.

2. Strain the stock to discard the meat, seasonings and vegetables. Add salt and pepper to taste. Refrigerate

the stock overnight. Separate or skim the fat from the

surface.

Nutrition: Calories: 12 Carbs: 2g Fat: 0g Protein: 1g

24. Corn Chili and Chicken

Preparation time: 15 minutes

Cooking time: 6-8 hours

Servings: 6

Ingredients:

- 2 large (or 4 small) chicken breasts or halves

- 1 (16 ounce) jar salsa

- 1 teaspoon chili powder

- 1 teaspoon ground cumin

- 2 teaspoons garlic powder

- 1 (15 ounce) can pinto beans

- 1 (11 ounce) can Mexican-style corn

- Salt and ground black pepper to taste

Directions:

1. Season the chicken and salsa with cumin powder, chili powder, salt, and ground pepper. Place in the crock pot.

2. Cook for 6 to 8 hours on low. Shred the chicken and return the meat to the Crockpot. Add the corn and the pinto beans into the Crockpot and simmer until hot. Serve.

Nutrition:

Calories: 188

Carbs: 23g

Fat: 2g

Protein: 20g

25. Chicken Drumsticks in Honey Sauce

Preparation time: 15 minutes

Cooking time: 4-5 hours

Servings: 4

Ingredients:

- 3 lb. chicken drumsticks

- 1 cup soy sauce

- 2 cups honey

- ¼ cup vegetable oil

- ½ cup spicy marinara sauce

- Salt and pepper to taste

Directions:

1. Put drumsticks on broiler pan and sprinkle wings with salt and pepper. Cook the drumsticks (sprinkled with salt and pepper) in the broiler until browned (15 minutes approximately). Flip over once in between.

2. Put the browned drumsticks in the Crockpot. Use another bowl to mix the soy sauce, honey, marinara, and oil. Pour over the drumsticks.

3. Cover Crockpot and turn heat to low. Cook for 4 to 5 hours. Serve hot.

Nutrition:

Calories: 195

Carbs: 18g

Fat: 7g

Protein: 17g

26. Orange Chicken & Sweet Potatoes

Preparation time: 15 minutes

Cooking time: 6-8 hours

Servings: 6

Ingredients:

- 6 pieces chicken thighs with the skin removed

- 4 cleaned and coarse cut sweet potatoes

- 1/2 cup chicken broth 1 cup orange marmalade

- Salt and pepper to taste

Directions:

1. Place the prepared sweet potatoes in the Crockpot, adding salt and pepper. Place the chicken thighs on top of sweet potatoes, adding salt and pepper again.

2. In separate bowl, mix the orange marmalade and chicken broth and pour over the chicken. Cover and cook on low for 6 to 8 hours. Pour a sauce of your choice and serve with steamed kale.

Nutrition: Calories: 240 Carbs: 48g Fat: 3g Protein: 3g

27. Chicken Breasts

Preparation time: 15 minutes

Cooking time: 8-10 hours

Servings: 5

Ingredients:

- 5 chicken breast halves, boned and skinned

- 4 medium baking potatoes, diced

- 2 medium onions, diced

- 2 tablespoon butter (can be substituted with margarine)

- 2 cans condensed cream of chicken soup with reduced fat,

- 1 teaspoon tarragon

- ½ cup dry sherry

- ¼ teaspoon garlic powder (can be substituted with garlic salt)

- 1 teaspoon Worcestershire sauce

- 1 can (4 ounce) mushrooms, drained properly

Directions:

1. First rinse and then pat dry the chicken breasts, place in crock pot, and add the potatoes and onions.

2. In a saucepan, put all the remaining components. Heat them until smooth and hot and then pour over chicken breasts. Cover and cook on low for 8 to 10 hours.

Nutrition:

Calories: 130

Carbs: 0g

Fat: 3g Protein: 24g

CHAPTER 6:

Meat

28.   Pork Chops and Mango

Preparation time: 10 minutes

Cooking time: 6 hours

Servings: 2

Ingredients:

- 1 pound pork chops

- 1 teaspoon sweet paprika

- ½ teaspoon chili powder

- 1 cup mango, peeled, and cubed

- 2 tablespoons ketchup

- 1 tablespoon balsamic vinegar

- ¼ cup beef stock

- 1 tablespoon cilantro, chopped

Directions:

1. In your crock pot, mix the pork chops with the paprika, chili powder, ketchup and the other ingredients, toss, put the lid on and cook on Low for 6 hours. Divide everything between plates and serve.

Nutrition:

Calories 345

Fat 5g

Carbs 17g Protein 14g

29.   Beef and Zucchinis Mix

Preparation time: 10 minutes Cooking time: 8 hours Servings: 2 Ingredients:

- 1 pound beef stew meat, cut into strips

- 1 tablespoon olive oil ¼ cup beef stock

- ½ teaspoon sweet paprika ½ teaspoon chili powder

- 2 small zucchinis, cubed 1 tablespoon balsamic vinegar

- 1 tablespoon chives, chopped

Directions:

1. In your crock pot, mix the beef with the oil, stock and the other ingredients, toss, put the lid on and cook on Low for 8 hours. Divide the mix between plates and serve.

Nutrition: Calories 400 Fat 12g Carbs 18g Protein 20g

30. Pork and Olives

Preparation time: 10 minutes

Cooking time: 8 hours Servings: 2

Ingredients:

- 1 pound pork roast, sliced ½ cup tomato passata

- 1 red onion, sliced 1 cup kalamata olives, pitted and halved

- Juice of ½ lime ¼ cup beef stock

- Salt and black pepper to the taste

- 1 tablespoon chives, hopped

Directions:

1. In your crock pot, mix the pork slices with the passata, onion, olives and the other ingredients, toss, put the lid

on and cook on Low for 8 hours. Divide the mix

between plates and serve.

Nutrition: Calories 360 Fat 4g Carbs 17g Protein 27g

31. Pork and Soy Sauce Mix

Preparation time: 10 minutes

Cooking time: 8 hours

Servings: 2

Ingredients:

- 1 pound pork loin roast, boneless and roughly cubed

- 1 tablespoon soy sauce

- 3 tablespoons honey

- ½ tablespoons oregano, dried

- 1 tablespoon garlic, minced

- 1 tablespoons olive oil

- Salt and black pepper to the taste

- ½ cup beef stock

- ½ teaspoon sweet paprika

Directions:

1. In your crock pot, mix the pork loin with the honey, soy sauce and the other ingredients, toss, put the lid on and cook on Low for 8 hours. Divide everything between plates and serve.

Nutrition:

Calories 374

Fat 6g

Carbs 29g

Protein 6g

Cooking time: 8 hours

Servings: 2

Ingredients:

- 1 pound beef stew meat, cubed

- 1 teaspoon garam masala

- ½ teaspoon turmeric powder

- Salt and black pepper to the taste

- 1 cup beef stock

- 1 teaspoon garlic, minced

- ½ cup sour cream

- 2 ounces cream cheese, soft

73

- 1 tablespoon chives, chopped

Directions:

1. In your crock pot, mix the beef with the turmeric, garam masala and the other ingredients, toss, put the lid on and cook on Low for 8 hours. Divide everything into bowls and serve.

Nutrition:

Calories 372

Fat 6g

Carbs 18g

Protein 22g

CHAPTER 7:

Vegetables

33.   Mac & Cheese

Preparation time: 20 minutes

Cooking time: 4 hours

Servings: 6

Ingredients:

- 16 oz elbow macaroni

- 16 oz shredded cheddar cheese

- 12 oz milk

- 4 eggs

- 1-1/2 cups cream

Directions:

1. Cook the macaroni until 'al dente' according to the package instructions.

2. Meanwhile, whisk together the milk, eggs, cream and 2/3 of the cheese, seasoning well with salt and pepper.

3. Stir the sauce through the cooked macaroni, and then pour the whole thing into your crock pot.

4. Sprinkle the remaining cheese all over the top of the macaroni mixture and cook on High for 3 hours, before reducing it to Low to cook for a 4 hour.

Nutrition:Calories: 315 Carbs: 44g Fat: 10g

Protein: 18g

34. Cauliflower Curry

Preparation time: 15 minutes

Cooking time: 4 hours

Servings: 6

Ingredients:

- 28 oz cauliflower florets

- 14 oz canned tomatoes

- 2 tablespoons ginger

- 1-1/2 tablespoons curry powder 1 onion

Directions:

1. Into the crock pot, add the canned tomatoes. Stir in the curry powder and ginger and a dash of salt and pepper.

2. Peel and dice the onion and chop the cauliflower into small florets and add everything into the crock pot too.

Cook on High for 4 hours until the cauliflower is nicely softened.

Nutrition:Calories: 475 Carbs: 45g Fat: 24g Protein: 26g

35.   Quinoa Stuffed Bell Peppers

Preparation time: 15 minutes

Cooking time: 3 hours

Servings: 6

Ingredients:

- 16 oz canned black beans

- 6 bell peppers

- 1-1/2 cups canned tomatoes

- 1-1/2 teaspoons chili powder

- 1 cup quinoa

Directions:

1. Chop the tops off of the peppers, and carefully scrape

   out the seeds. Blend the canned tomatoes into a sauce.

2. Drain the beans and mix them together with the quinoa, canned tomatoes and chili powder. Season well with salt and pepper.

3. Divide the quinoa mixture evenly between the peppers. Into the bottom of the crock pot, pour ½ of a cup of water. Then, place the peppers in so that they're sitting in the water. Cook on High for 3 hours.

Nutrition:

Calories: 598

Carbs: 86g

Fat: 18g

Protein: 28g

36.   Garlic Hoisin Mushrooms

Preparation time: 15 minutes

Cooking time: 3 hours

Servings: 6

Ingredients:

- 24 of fresh button mushrooms

- 6 garlic cloves

- 1/2 cup hoisin sauce

- 1/2 teaspoon chili flakes

Directions:

1. Mince the garlic and mix it together with the hoisin sauce, chili flakes and ¼ of a cup of water. Peel the mushrooms and rinse them, and then add them into the crock pot.

2. Pour the sauce all over the mushrooms and stir well to coat them and season with salt and pepper. Cook on High for 3 hours.

Nutrition: Calories: 51 Carbs: 9g Fat: 1g Protein: 3g

CHAPTER 8:

Soups & Stews

37.   White Bean and Barley Soup

Preparation time: 15 minutes

Cooking time: 6 hours

Servings: 8

Ingredients:

- 2 (15-ounce) cans great northern beans, drained and rinsed

- ½ cup pearl barley

- ½ onion, diced

- 2 carrots, peeled and diced

- 2 cloves garlic, minced

- ¼ cup fresh parsley, chopped

- 2 sprigs fresh thyme

- 6 cups vegetable broth

- 1½ tsp. salt

Directions:

1. Add everything in the crock pot and cover. Cook on low for 6 hours. Remove thyme and serve.

Nutrition:

Calories 182.5

Carbs 3g

Fat 1g

Protein 8g

38.   Red Lentil Soup

Preparation time: 15 minutes

Cooking time: 6 hours & 3 minutes

Servings: 6

Ingredients:

- 2 cups red lentils, rinsed

- 3 tbsps. butter

- 1 small onion, sliced

- 1½ tsps. fresh ginger, peeled and minced

- 2 cloves garlic, minced

- 6 cups vegetable Broth

- Juice of 1 lemon

- ½ tsp. paprika

- 1 tsp. cayenne pepper

- 1½ tsps. salt

Directions:

1. Press the Sauté and add butter. Cook onion, garlic, and ginger for 3 minutes. Then add everything and cover. Cook on low for 6 hours. Serve.

Nutrition:

Calories 296

Carbs 54g

Fat 10g

Protein 18g

39. French Onion Soup

Preparation time: 15 minutes

Cooking time: 4 hours & 4 minutes

Servings: 4

Ingredients:

- ¼ cup olive oil

- 4 Vidalia onions, sliced

- 4 cloves garlic, minced

- 1 tbsp. dried thyme

- 1 cup red wine

- 4 cups vegetable broth

- 1 tsp. salt

- 1 tsp. pepper

- 4 slices French bread

- 4 ounces Swiss cheese

Directions:

1. Heat the oil on Sauté. Cook onions for 3 minutes. Add garlic and sauté for 1 minute. Add everything and cover. Cook on low for 4 hours.

2. Meanwhile, preheat the oven to broiler. Lightly toast the bread slices. Ladle the soup into the bowls. Place a slice of toasted bread on top of the soup.

3. Put a slice of cheese on top. Broil until cheese has melted. Serve.

Nutrition:

Calories 471

Carbs 45g

Fat 22g Protein 14g

40. Artichoke Soup

Preparation time: 15 minutes

Cooking time: 5 hours

Servings: 2

Ingredients:

- 2 cups canned (drained and halved) artichoke hearts

- 1 small carrot, chopped

- 1 small yellow onion, chopped

- 1 garlic clove, minced

- ¼ tsp. oregano, dried

- ¼ tsp. rosemary, dried

- A pinch of red pepper flakes

- A pinch of garlic powder

- A pinch of salt and black pepper

- 3 cups veggie stock

- 1 tbsp. tomato paste

- 1 tbsp. cilantro, chopped

Directions:

1. Mix everything in the crock pot and cover. Cook on low for 5 hours. Serve.

Nutrition:

Calories 362

Carbs 16g

Fat 3g

Protein 5g

41.   Beer Cheese Soup

Preparation time: 15 minutes

Cooking time: 4 hours & 10 minutes

Servings: 12

Ingredients:

- ½ cup butter

- ½ white onion, diced

- 2 medium carrots, peeled and diced

- 2 ribs celery, diced

- ½ cup flour

- 3 cups vegetable broth

- 1 (12-ounce) beer bottle

- 3 cups of milk

- 3 cups cheddar cheese

- 1 tsp. salt

- 1 tsp. pepper

- ½ tsp. dry ground mustard

Directions:

1. In the crock pot, melt the butter on Sauté. Add onion, carrots, and celery and cook for 5 to 7 minutes. Add the flour and mix.

2. Cook for 3 minutes. Add everything in the crock pot and mix. Cover and cook on low for 4 hours. Open and serve.

Nutrition:

Calories 275

Carbs 1g Fat 19g Protein 10.5g

CHAPTER 9:

Snacks

42. Spicy Pecans

Preparation Time: 10 minutes   Cooking Time: 3 hours

Servings: 16   Ingredients:

- 3 lbs. pecan halves   2 tbsp. Cajun seasoning blend   2 tbsp. olive oil

Directions:

1. Add all ingredients to the crock pot and stir well to combine. Cover crock pot with lid and cook on low for

1 hour. Stir well. Cover again and cook for 2 hours more. Serve and enjoy.

Nutrition: Calories 607   Fat 62.5 g   Carbs 12.2 g   Protein 9.1 g

43.   Seasoned Mixed Nuts

Preparation Time: 10 minutes

Cooking Time: 2 hours   Servings: 20

Ingredients:

- 8 cups mixed nuts   3 tbsp. curry powder

- 4 tbsp. butter, melted   Salt

Directions:

1. Add all ingredients into the crock pot and stir well to combine. Cover crock pot with lid and cook on high for a ½ hour.

2. Stir again and cook for 30 minutes more. Cover again and cook on low for 1 hour more. Stir well and serve.

Nutrition:

Calories 375   Fat 34.7 g   Carbs 12.8 g   Protein 9 g

44. Nacho Cheese Dip

Preparation Time: 10 minutes   Cooking Time: 2 hours

Servings: 8

Ingredients:

- 8 oz. cream cheese, cut into chunks

- ¼ cup almond milk

- ½ cup chunky salsa

- 1 cup cheddar cheese, shredded

Directions:

1. Add all ingredients to the crock pot and stir well. Cover crock pot with lid and cook on low for 2 hours. Stir to mix. Serve with fresh vegetables.

Nutrition: Calories 178 Fat 16.4 g Carbs 2.4 g Protein 6.1 g

45.   Cheese Chicken Dip

Preparation Time: 10 minutes

Cooking Time: 2 hours

Servings: 10

Ingredients:

- ½ cup bell peppers, chopped

- 1 cup chicken breast, cooked and shredded

- 12 oz. can tomato with green chilies

- ½ lb. cheese, cubed

Directions:

1. Add all ingredients into the crock pot and stir well to combine. Cover crock pot with lid and cook on low for 2 hours. Stir well and serve.

Nutrition: Calories 120   Fat 8 g   Carbs 2 g   Protein 10 g

46. Mexican Cheese Dip

Preparation Time: 10 minutes   Cooking Time: 1 hour

Servings: 6   Ingredients:

- 1 tsp. taco seasoning

- ¾ cup tomatoes with green chilies

- 8 oz. Velveeta cheese, cut into cube

Directions:

1. Add cheese into the crock pot. Cover and cook on low for 30 minutes. Stir occasionally. Add taco seasoning and tomatoes with green chilies and stir well.

2. Cover again and cook on low for 30 minutes more. Stir well and serve.

Nutrition: Calories 159   Fat 12.6 g   Carbs 1.9 g   Protein 9.6 g

CHAPTER 10:

Desserts

47.   Gooey Fudge Cake

Preparation time: 5 minutes

Cooking time: 1 hour & 30 minutes

Servings: 4

Ingredients:

Fudge Ingredients:

- 1 box (15¼ ounces) Betty Crocker Chocolate Fudge Cake mix

- 1 box (4 ounces) Jell-O Chocolate Instant Pudding Mix

- 4 eggs

- 2/3 cup sour cream

- ¾ cup vegetable oil

- Non-stick cooking spray

Optional Toppings:

- 1 jar hot fudge sauce

- 1 scoop vanilla ice cream

Directions:

1. Grease a crockpot and mix the fudge ingredients together with an electric or hand mixer until everything is fully blended.

2. Pour the mixture into the crockpot and cook everything on high for 1½ hours. Scoop some fudge

into a bowl and top with optional toppings, if desired.

Serve and enjoy.

Nutrition:Calories 360 Fat 8 g Carbs 64 g Protein 8 g

48. Pumpkin Cake

Preparation time: 5 minutes

Cooking time: 1 hour & 30 minutes

Servings: 4

Ingredients:

- 1 box (15¼ ounces) Betty Crocker Spice Cake Mix

- 1 can (15 ounces) Libby's Pure Pumpkin

- ½ cup applesauce

- 3 eggs

- 1 teaspoon pumpkin pie spice

- Non-stick cooking spray

Optional Garnish:

- 2 teaspoons pumpkin pie spice

- 2 teaspoons ground cinnamon

- Cream cheese frosting

Directions:

1. Whisk all of the ingredients in a bowl using an electric or hand mixer. Grease a crock pot and then pour the mixture into it.

2. Cook everything on high for 1½ to 2 hours. Cut the cake into serving-sized pieces and transfer to plates. Top with the optional garnish and serve.

Nutrition:

Calories 200

Fat 5 g

Carbs 34 g

Protein 6 g

49.   Spiced Apple Surprise

Preparation time: 5 minutes

Cooking time: 2 hours

Servings: 8

Ingredients:

- 42 ounces apple pie filling, canned or homemade

- 1 box (15¼ ounces) Betty Crocker Spice Cake Mix

- 1 stick butter, melted

- 2 teaspoons ground cinnamon

- Non-stick cooking spray

Optional Toppings:

- 1 scoop ice cream

- 1 dollop whipped cream

Directions:

1. Grease a crockpot and then evenly cover the bottom with the pie filling. Mix the cake mix and melted butter in a bowl with a wooden spoon. Make sure that no large chunks remain.

2. Sprinkle the cinnamon evenly over the apple filling, then top with the cake mix mixture. Cook everything on high for 2 hours.

3. Transfer everything to plates, top with your preferred toppings, and serve.

Nutrition:

Calories 434

Fat 20 g

Carbs 58 g

Protein 8 g

50.   Lemon Cake Squares

Preparation time: 15 minutes

Cooking time: 1 hour & 30 minutes

Servings: 4

Ingredients:

Cake Ingredients:

- 1 box (15¼ ounces) Betty Crocker Lemon Cake Mix

- ½ cup applesauce

- 1 1/3 cups water

- 3 eggs

Toppings:

- Cream cheese frosting

- 1 teaspoon lemon juice

Directions:

1. Grease a crock pot and whisk all the cake ingredients together with an electric or hand mixer. Pour the mixture into the crock pot and cook everything on high for 1½ to 2 hours.

2. When the cake is almost done cooking, mix the topping ingredients together and cover with cling wrap. Cut the cake into bite-sized squares and coat with the topping mixture. Serve and enjoy.

Nutrition:

Calories 130

Fat 6 g

Carbs 15 g

Protein 0 g

Conclusion

You have to the end of this amazing cookbook, but always remember that this is not the end of your cooking journey with the crockpot; but instead, this is your stepping stone towards more cooking glory. We hope you have found your favorite recipes that are time-saving and money-saving.

Now that you know how Crockpot works and the many benefits of using it, maybe it is time for you to buy one for your family, in case you haven't owned one. When it comes to time spent preparing meals for your family, Crock-Pot is a lifesaver. If you are a busy person, a powerful solution is to use the crockpot.

You will also love to own one if you want to make your life simpler at work if you want to make your life simpler at home, and if you want to preserve some of the natural resources. You could also use one if you want to lean towards a healthier lifestyle as cooking in the crockpot is conducive to health than in the oven.

The crockpot can be used in making homemade and custom-made buffets, even in catering services. You can use it for cooking for your staff for special occasions and for showing them how to cook a tasty and healthier dish for your guests well within their own crockpot.

After choosing the best one for you, maybe it is time for you to know more about the recipes you should use. There are various recipes in this cookbook that are perfect for crockpot cooking, and they will definitely be useful and beneficial for you.

Moreover, whether you are a newbie or an experienced cook, you are going to love this cookbook as it is packed with every conceivable taste. You have discovered more than 1000 recipes in this cookbook that you can put into practice using your crockpot. You can always customize the recipes to suit your taste buds, as you can make any recipe mild or hot, sweet or sour; you have all the freedom to make the recipes your own. The best thing about cooking using a crockpot is that you just need to add the main ingredients, and no other complicated cooking preparation is needed; the crockpot will add most of the other ingredients for you.

This crockpot cookbook covered all the recipes that are sure to make your heart happy and your taste buds happy as well. These meals are not just easy to make, but they will also save you hours of preparation and cleanup. The crockpot is also famous for its great nutritional value. It is the best nutritional value you will ever get. The high levels of healthy fats, proteins, and fiber you get when you cook using the crockpot are entirely natural, which everybody needs. Some of the ingredients are healthy enough to be consumed on their own.

CPSIA information can be obtained
at www.ICGtesting.com
Printed in the USA
BVHW080935260421
605870BV00016B/644